GW01377183

LOW PURINE DIET

MEGA BUNDLE – 3 Manuscripts in 1 – 120+ Low purine - friendly recipes including casseroles, side dishes and pizza

TABLE OF CONTENTS

ROAST RECIPES 9
ROASTED ONION 9
ROASTED SQUASH 10
ROASTED GARLIC 11
SOUP RECIPES 12
ZUCCHINI SOUP 12
CREAMY CAULIFLOWER SOUP 13
SWEET POTATO SOUP 14
SIDE DISHES 15
GREEN PESTO PASTA 15
FAJITA LETTUCE WRAPS 16
FAJITAS WITH BASIL SAUCE 18
BRUSEELS SPROUTS WITH BALSAMIC GLAZE 20
ROASTED SWEET POTATOES 22
SPAGHETTI SQUASH PLATTER 23
ROASTED CAULIFLOWER AND RICE PLATTER 25
SALAD WITH KALE CAULIFLOWER 26
GRAIN FREE FAJITAS 28
LIME SPINACH CHIPS 30
AIP BREADSTICKS 31
CAULIFLOWER RICE 33
GLAZED SALMON 34
BISON STEW 35
GARLIC AND HERB SCALLOPS 36
ROASTED ROSEMARY BEETS 37
BACON-WRAPPED SHRIMP 38
PORK CHOPS WITH ONION 39

BACON & KALE	40
GREEK SALAD	41
QUINOA AND LENTIL SALAD	42
CRANBERRY & SPINACH SALAD	43
KALE SALAD	44
TORTELLINI SALAD	45
TACO SALAD	46
DORITO TACO SALAD	47
CHEESEBURGER SALAD	48
MANDARIN SALAD	49
SOUTHWESTERN SALAD	50
STEW RECIPES	51
BUTTERNUT SQUASH STEW	51
BEEF STEW	53
CASSEROLE RECIPES	55
CORN CASSEROLE	55
ARTICHOKE CASSEROLE	57
PIZZA RECIPES	58
MUSHROOM PIZZA	58
CASSEROLE PIZZA	60
SECOND COOKBOOK	61
BREAKFAST RECIPES	62
MUSHROOM OMELETTE	62
AVOCADO TOAST	64
TOMATO SHAKSHUKA	65
PORTOBELLO MUSHROOM CAPS	67
EGG IN AVOCADO	68
OMELETTE BITES	69

MACADAMIA WAFFLES	71
BACON & AVOCADO SANDWICHES	72
ZUCCHINI FRITTATA	73
SWEET POTATO BREAKFAST CAKE	74
MINI EGG OMELETS	76
BREAKFAST MEATCAKES	77
CANTALOUPE PANCAKES	79
COCONUT PANCAKES	80
CHERRIES PANCAKES	81
MANGO MUFFINS	82
NECTARINE MUFFINS	83
PAPAYA MUFFINS	84
PLANTAIN MUFFINS	85
ONION OMELETTE	86
BEETROOT OMELETTE	87
BELL PEPPER OMELETTE	88
TART RECIPES	89
PEAR TART	89
CARDAMOM TART	91
PIE RECIPES	93
PEACH PECAN PIE	93
BUTTERFINGER PIE	94
STRAWBERRY PIE	95
BLUEBERRY PIE	96
SMOOTHIE RECIPES	97
GINGER-OAT SMOOTHIE	97
PUMPKIN SMOOTHIE	98
GREEN SMOOTHIE	99

MANGO SMOOTHIE	100
PINEAPPLE SMOOTHIE	101
CASHEW SMOOTHIE	102
NUT SMOOTHIE	103
STRAWBERRY SMOOTHIE	104
SPINACH & GRAPE SMOOTHIE	105
ICE-CREAM RECIPES	106
SAFFRON ICE-CREAM	106
PISTACHIOS ICE-CREAM	108
VANILLA ICE-CREAM	109
THIRD COOKBOOK	110
SOUP RECIPES	111
ZUCCHINI SOUP	111
BROCCOLI SOUP	112
CHICKEN NOODLE SOUP	114
TORTILLA SOUP	116
ASPARAGUS SOUP	117
LENTIL SOUP	118
BROCCOLI AND RED CAPSICUM SOUP	120
CANTALOUPE SOUP	121
SIDE DISHES	122
GREEN PESTO PASTA	122
BUCKWHEAT DOSA	123
ZUCCHINI BAJRA KHICHDI	124
QUINOA MUTHIA	126
LIME GRILLED CORN	128
CAPSICUM AND PANEER SUBZI	129
AVOCADO DIP	131

ONION PURIS	132
KALE CHIPS	133
CRANBERRY SALAD	134
ITALIAN SALAD	135
CHICKPEA COLESLAW	136
ROMAINE SALAD	137
GRAIN SALAD	138
QUINOA SALAD	139
WEDGE SALAD	140
COUSCOUS SALAD	141
FARRO SALAD	142
THAI MANGO SALAD	143
LENTIL FRITATTA	144
SPINACH FRITATTA	145
BLACK BEAN FRITATTA	146
CHEESE FRITATTA	147
BROCCOLI FRITATTA	148
SHAKSHUKA	149
BROCCOLI CASSEROLE	150
BEAN FRITATTA	151
ROASTED SQUASH	152
POTATO CHIPS	153
ZUCCHINI CHIPS	154
PIZZA RECIPES	**155**
ZUCCHINI PIZZA CRUST	155
BARBEQUE PIZZA	157
SHRIMP PIZZA	158
CAULIFLOWER CRUST PIZZA	159

Copyright 2020 by Noah Jerris - All rights reserved.

This document is geared towards providing exact and reliable information in regards to the topic and issue covered. The publication is sold with the idea that the publisher is not required to render accounting, officially permitted, or otherwise, qualified services. If advice is necessary, legal or professional, a practiced individual in the profession should be ordered.

- From a Declaration of Principles which was accepted and approved equally by a Committee of the American Bar Association and a Committee of Publishers and Associations.

In no way is it legal to reproduce, duplicate, or transmit any part of this document in either electronic means or in printed format. Recording of this publication is strictly prohibited and any storage of this document is not allowed unless with written permission from the publisher. All rights reserved.

The information provided herein is stated to be truthful and consistent, in that any liability, in terms of inattention or otherwise, by any usage or abuse of any policies, processes, or directions contained within is the solitary and utter responsibility of the recipient reader. Under no circumstances will any legal responsibility or blame be held against the publisher for any reparation, damages, or monetary loss due to the information herein, either directly or indirectly.

Respective authors own all copyrights not held by the publisher.

The information herein is offered for informational purposes solely, and is universal as so. The presentation of the information is without contract or any type of guarantee assurance.

The trademarks that are used are without any consent, and the publication of the trademark is without permission or backing by the trademark owner. All trademarks and brands within this book are for clarifying purposes only and are the owned by the owners themselves, not affiliated with this document.

Introduction

Low Purine recipes for personal enjoyment but also for family enjoyment. You will love them for sure for how easy it is to prepare them.

ROAST RECIPES

ROASTED ONION

Serves: **3-4**

Prep Time: **10** Minutes

Cook Time: **20** Minutes

Total Time: **30** Minutes

INGREDIENTS

- 1 lb. onion
- 2 tablespoons olive oil
- 1 tsp curry powder
- 1 tsp salt

DIRECTIONS

1. Preheat the oven to 400 F
2. Cut everything in half lengthwise
3. Toss everything with olive oil and place onto a prepared baking sheet
4. Roast for 18-20 minutes at 400 F or until golden brown
5. When ready remove from the oven and serve

ROASTED SQUASH

Serves: **3-4**

Prep Time: **10** Minutes

Cook Time: **20** Minutes

Total Time: **30** Minutes

INGREDIENTS

- 2 delicata squashes
- 2 tablespoons olive oil
- 1 tsp curry powder
- 1 tsp salt

DIRECTIONS

1. Preheat the oven to 400 F
2. Cut everything in half lengthwise
3. Toss everything with olive oil and place onto a prepared baking sheet
4. Roast for 18-20 minutes at 400 F or until golden brown
5. When ready remove from the oven and serve

ROASTED GARLIC

Serves: **2**

Prep Time: **10** Minutes

Cook Time: **10** Minutes

Total Time: **20** Minutes

INGREDIENTS

- 1 head garlic
- 1 tablespoon olive oil

DIRECTIONS

1. Preheat oven to 375 F
2. Ove the garlic drizzle the olive oil and add to the pan
3. Roast for 15-20 minutes and remove from the oven
4. Let it cool and serve

SOUP RECIPES

ZUCCHINI SOUP

Serves: **4**
Prep Time: **10** Minutes
Cook Time: **20** Minutes
Total Time: **30** Minutes

INGREDIENTS

- 1 tablespoon olive oil
- 1 lb. zucchini
- ¼ red onion
- ½ cup all-purpose flour
- ¼ tsp salt
- ¼ tsp pepper
- 1 can vegetable broth
- 1 cup heavy cream

DIRECTIONS

1. In a saucepan heat olive oil and sauté zucchini until tender
2. Add remaining ingredients to the saucepan and bring to a boil
3. When all the vegetables are tender transfer to a blender and blend until smooth
4. Pour soup into bowls, garnish with parsley and serve

CREAMY CAULIFLOWER SOUP

Serves: **3**

Prep Time: **10** Minutes

Cook Time: **50** Minutes

Total Time: **60** Minutes

INGREDIENTS

- 1 head cauliflower
- 1 apple
- 1 tablespoon olive oil
- 2 cups almond milk
- 1 tablespoon fresh basil
- 1 tsp curry powder
- 1 tsp sesame seeds

DIRECTIONS

1. Preheat oven to 350 F and place the cauliflower on a prepared baking sheet
2. Drizzle with salt, pepper and olive oil
3. Roast for 40-45 minutes and remove from the oven
4. In a blender mix the cauliflower with the rest of the ingredients until smooth
5. Season with sesame seeds and serve

SWEET POTATO SOUP

Serves: 3

Prep Time: 10 Minutes

Cook Time: 50 Minutes

Total Time: 60 Minutes

INGREDIENTS

- 1 sweet potato
- 1 tsp olive oil
- 1 lbs. cranberries
- ½ cup water
- 1 tablespoon cashew butter
- 1 tsp salt

DIRECTIONS

1. Preheat oven to 350 F and place the potatoes on a baking sheet, rub them with olive oil and roast for 45-50 minutes
2. Meanwhile cook the cranberries until tender, remove from the heat when ready
3. Remove the sweet potato from the oven and place blend it in a blender with cranberries and cashew butter and salt
4. Pour in a bowl and serve

SIDE DISHES

GREEN PESTO PASTA

Serves: 2

Prep Time: 5 Minutes

Cook Time: 15 Minutes

Total Time: 20 Minutes

INGREDIENTS

- 4 oz. spaghetti
- 2 cups basil leaves
- 2 garlic cloves
- ¼ cup olive oil
- 2 tablespoons parmesan cheese
- ½ tsp black pepper

DIRECTIONS

1. Bring water to a boil and add pasta
2. In a blend add parmesan cheese, basil leaves, garlic and blend
3. Add olive oil, pepper and blend again
4. Pour pesto onto pasta and serve when ready

FAJITA LETTUCE WRAPS

Serves: **2**

Prep Time: **10** Minutes

Cook Time: **10** Minutes

Total Time: **20** Minutes

INGREDIENTS

- 2 tablespoons olive oil
- 1 onion
- ¼ cumin
- ¼ cup tomatoes
- 1 tablespoon walnuts
- 2 tablespoons parsley
- 3 carrots
- 1 zucchini
- ¼ tsp salt
- ¼ tsp pepper
- ¼ tsp cinnamon

DIRECTIONS

1. In a skillet sauté the olive oil and onion over low heat
2. Add carrots and zucchini and cook for 5-6 minutes
3. Add cinnamon, pepper and salt and cook for 1-2 minutes

4. Spoon into lettuce leaves and add walnuts, parsley and tomatoes

FAJITAS WITH BASIL SAUCE

Serves: **2**

Prep Time: **10** Minutes

Cook Time: **20** Minutes

Total Time: **30** Minutes

INGREDIENTS

- ½ cup quinoa
- 1 cup water
- ½ cup onion
- 1 tablespoon parsley
- 1 tsp lemon zest
- 6 tortillas
- 1 can cannellini beans
- 1 pint cheery tomatoes
- 1 cucumber

Basil sauce

- 8 tomatillos
- 2 tablespoons cannellini beans
- 1 cucumber
- 1 tablespoon almond butter
- 3 basil leaves

DIRECTIONS

1. Hold tortilla over flame to low heat for 3-4 seconds each side
2. Cook quinoa for 10-15 minutes and remove form heat
3. Puree the basil sauce ingredients in a blender
4. Season with salt and pepper and serve

BRUSEELS SPROUTS WITH BALSAMIC GLAZE

Serves: **3**

Prep Time: **10** Minutes

Cook Time: **40** Minutes

Total Time: **50** Minutes

INGREDIENTS

- 1 head garlic
- 1 lbs. Brussels sprouts
- 1 tablespoon olive oil
- 1 kale
- ½ cup cabbage
- 1 tablespoon almonds
- 1 tsp lemon zest
- 1 tablespoon cherries

Balsamic Glaze
- ½ cup tahini
- 1 tablespoon balsamic vinegar
- 1 tablespoon lemon juice
- salt
- pepper

DIRECTIONS

1. Preheat oven to 375 F and place a baking sheet with parchment paper
2. Slice the garlic and drizzle it and Brussels sprouts with oil, salt and pepper
3. Place them on the baking sheet and roast for 25-30 minutes, remove them when ready
4. Drizzle with balsamic glaze (mix all the ingredients in a bowl)

ROASTED SWEET POTATOES

Serves: **4**

Prep Time: **10** Minutes

Cook Time: **50** Minutes

Total Time: **60** Minutes

INGREDIENTS

- 2 sweet potatoes
- 1 tsp olive oil

Sauce

- ½ avocado diced
- ¼ peach halves
- 3 basil leaves
- 1 tablespoon red onion
- 2 tablespoons water
- ¼ navel orange juiced

DIRECTIONS

1. Preheat the oven to 375 F and place the sweet potatoes on a baking sheet
2. Rub them with olive oil and roast for 40-45 minutes and remove from oven when ready
3. For sauce combine all the ingredients in a blender

SPAGHETTI SQUASH PLATTER

Serves: **3**

Prep Time: **10** Minutes

Cook Time: **40** Minutes

Total Time: **50** Minutes

INGREDIENTS

- 1 spaghetti squash
- 1 tablespoon onion
- 1 avocado peeled
- 1 whole pear
- 1 tablespoon cashews
- 1 tablespoon nuts
- 1 tablespoon cherries
- 1 tablespoon fresh dill
- 1 tsp sesame seeds
- 1 tablespoon olive oil
- 1 cucumber

Tahini Garlic Dressing

- ½ cup tahini
- 1 clove garlic
- ¼ cup water

DIRECTIONS

1. Preheat oven to 350 F and place squash on a baking sheet and drizzle with olive oil and salt
2. Roast for 40-45 minutes and remove from oven when ready
3. Scoop out the spaghetti squash except the sesame seeds and dill
4. Mix all the ingredients in a bowl and drizzle over the squash and sprinkle with the dill

ROASTED CAULIFLOWER AND RICE PLATTER

Serves: **4**

Prep Time: **10** Minutes

Cook Time: **30** Minutes

Total Time: **40** Minutes

INGREDIENTS

- 1 large head cauliflower
- 1 red pepper
- 2 tablespoons red onion
- 1 tablespoon macadamia nuts
- 1 scallion
- 1 fresh basil leave
- 1 can sardines
- 1 tablespoon olive oil
- ½ cup wild rice

DIRECTIONS

1. Preheat oven to 375 F and line a baking sheet
2. Place the cauliflower on the baking sheet and drizzle with olive oil and salt
3. Roast for 20-25 minutes and remove when ready
4. Cook the rice and place it on a platter and add the cauliflower, season with salt and serve

SALAD WITH KALE CAULIFLOWER

Serves: 2

Prep Time: 10 Minutes

Cook Time: 20 Minutes

Total Time: 30 Minutes

INGREDIENTS

- 1 head cauliflower
- 1 cup arugula
- 1 tablespoon sunflower seeds
- ¼ cup tahini
- 1 garlic clove
- 1 tablespoon olive oil
- 1 head purple kale
- 1 cup cherry tomatoes
- 1 head cabbage
- 1 cup green grapes

DIRECTIONS

1. Preheat the oven to 375 F and place the cauliflower on a baking sheet and drizzle with olive oil and salt
2. Roast for 20-25 minutes and remove when ready
3. In a bowl combine cabbage, grapes, arugula, sunflower seeds, kale and tomatoes

4. In bowl mix tahini and garlic clove and drizzle over the salad

GRAIN FREE FAJITAS

Serves: **3**

Prep Time: **10** Minutes

Cook Time: **10** Minutes

Total Time: **20** Minutes

INGREDIENTS

- 1 tablespoon avocado oil
- 3 carrots
- 3 large nori sheets
- 1 tomato
- 1 tablespoon fresh cilantro
- 1 red pepper
- 1 green bell pepper
- 1 while onion
- 1 jalapeno

DIRECTIONS

1. In a skillet sauce avocado oil, onion, jalapeno, white onion, salt and pepper for 6-7 minutes
2. Remove from heat and place mixture in a bowl
3. Sauté carrots with pepper and salt for 5-6 minutes
4. Combine coconut milk with curry powder and combine with red onion, sea s alt and pepper

5. Lay the nori sheets and top with pepper mixture and carrots and drizzle with coconut milk

LIME SPINACH CHIPS

Serves: **6**

Prep Time: **10** Minutes

Cook Time: **30** Minutes

Total Time: **40** Minutes

INGREDIENTS

- 1 whole lime
- ¼ tsp salt
- 6 cups spinach
- 2 tablespoons olive oil

DIRECTIONS

1. In a bowl toss the spinach with olive oil and lime juice
2. Add salt, and distribute the spinach evenly onto a cookie sheet
3. Bake for 30 minutes at 300 F
4. When ready remove from the oven and serve

AIP BREADSTICKS

Serves: **6-8**

Prep Time: **10** Minutes

Cook Time: **15** Minutes

Total Time: **25** Minutes

INGREDIENTS

- 4 tablespoons olive oil
- 2 tablespoons water
- ½ cup coconut flour
- ¼ tsp baking soda
- 1 tsp rosemary
- 1 tsp lemon juice
- 1 tablespoon unflavored gelatin
- ¼ tsp garlic powder
- ¼ tsp salt

DIRECTIONS

1. Preheat oven to 325 F
2. In a blender add gelatin, 1 tablespoon of water, and blend
3. Add the rest of ingredients and blend until it thickens
4. Remove dough and divide into 6-8 portions
5. Grease each ball with olive oil and form small sticks

6. Sprinkle garlic, salt and rosemary on each one
7. Bake at 325 F for 12-15 minutes
8. When ready remove from the oven and serve

CAULIFLOWER RICE

Serves: **4**

Prep Time: **10** Minutes

Cook Time: **15** Minutes

Total Time: **25** Minutes

INGREDIENTS

- 1 clove garlic
- 1 tablespoon olive oil
- 1 head cauliflower
- ¼ cup yellow onion
- ¼ tsp salt
- 1 tsp herb seasoning

DIRECTIONS

1. Grate the cauliflower and place it in a blender
2. Blend until smooth
3. In a skillet heat coconut oil
4. Sauté garlic, onion and cauliflower for 4-5 minutes
5. Season with salt, pepper and serve

GLAZED SALMON

Serves: 2

Prep Time: **10** Minutes

Cook Time: **25** Minutes

Total Time: **35** Minutes

INGREDIENTS

- 12 oz. salmon filet
- 1 tablespoon maple syrup
- 1 tablespoon coconut aminos
- 1 tablespoon olive oil

DIRECTIONS

1. **Preheat the oven to 325 F**
2. **In a saucepan add maple syrup, coconut aminos and olive oil and stir until a glaze has formed**
3. **Place salmon filet on a baking sheet and brush with glaze**
4. **Bake for 20-25 minutes or until the fish is tender**
5. **When ready remove from heat and serve**

BISON STEW

Serves: **6**

Prep Time: **10** Minutes

Cook Time: **50** Minutes

Total Time: **60** Minutes

INGREDIENTS

- 2 lb. bison steak
- 1 tablespoon coconut oil
- 2 cups celery
- 2 sprig thyme
- 1 head cauliflower
- 1 onion
- 1-quart beef broth
- ¼ tsp salt

DIRECTIONS

1. In a skillet brown the stew on both sides and transfer to a pot
2. In the pot add celery, onion and beef broth
3. Add celery, thyme, cauliflower and bring to a boil
4. Simmer for 40-50 minutes or until the stew is completely cooked

GARLIC AND HERB SCALLOPS

Serves: **4**

Prep Time: **10** Minutes

Cook Time: **15** Minutes

Total Time: **25** Minutes

INGREDIENTS

- ¼ cup water
- 1 tablespoon olive oil
- 1 tablespoon lemon juice
- ¼ tsp salt
- ¼ tsp onion powder
- ¼ tsp garlic
- 4 oz. scallops
- 1 cup kale
- 1 tablespoon salad dressing

DIRECTIONS

1. In a pot toss scallop with salad dressing
2. Place scallops in a steamer with all vegetables and steam for 12-15 minutes
3. Remove from pot and place vegetables on a plate
4. Add lemon juice, seasoning and serve

ROASTED ROSEMARY BEETS

Serves: 2

Prep Time: 10 Minutes

Cook Time: 35 Minutes

Total Time: 45 Minutes

INGREDIENTS

- 2 tablespoons olive oil
- 2 tablespoons rosemary
- 2 beets
- ¼ salt

DIRECTIONS

1. Preheat the oven to 375 F
2. Brush beets with olive oil, sprinkle with salt and rosemary
3. Place the beets in a baking dish
4. Roast beets for 30-35 minutes
5. When ready remove from the oven and serve

BACON-WRAPPED SHRIMP

Serves: *8*
Prep Time: *10* Minutes
Cook Time: *30* Minutes
Total Time: *40* Minutes

INGREDIENTS

- 1 lb. shrimp
- 12 oz. bacon

DIRECTIONS

1. Cut bacon in half and wrap each shrimp with bacon
2. Skewer each shrimp and place the skewers on a baking sheet
3. Cook for 25-30 minutes
4. When ready remove from the oven and serve

PORK CHOPS WITH ONION

Serves: **4**

Prep Time: **10** Minutes

Cook Time: **20** Minutes

Total Time: **30** Minutes

INGREDIENTS

- 2 tablespoons lard
- 1 lb. pork chops
- ¼ onion
- 1 tsp fennel
- ¼ tsp salt
- Juice of 1 lemon

DIRECTIONS

1. In a skillet add the onions and cook until soft
2. Season pork chops with salt and fennel
3. Place the pork chops in the skillet and cook for 5-6 minutes per side
4. Remove pork chops from the pan and set aside
5. Add lemon juice, parsley and pour mixture over pork chops, serve when ready

BACON & KALE

Serves: **4**
Prep Time: **5** Minutes
Cook Time: **10** Minutes
Total Time: **15** Minutes

INGREDIENTS

- 1 bunch kale
- 2 oz. bacon
- ½ cup broth
- 1 tablespoon lemon juice
- 1 clove garlic

DIRECTIONS

1. Place the bacon in a skillet and cook until crispy
2. Add broth, kale, and cook until broth has evaporated
3. Add garlic, lemon juice and stir for 1-2 minutes
4. When ready remove and serve

GREEK SALAD

Serves: *2*

Prep Time: *5* Minutes

Cook Time: *5* Minutes

Total Time: *10* Minutes

INGREDIENTS

- 1 cup cherry tomatoes
- 1 cucumber
- 1 cup olives
- ½ cup onion
- 1 cup feta
- 1 cup salad dressing

DIRECTIONS

1. **In a bowl mix all ingredients and mix well**
2. **Serve with dressing**

QUINOA AND LENTIL SALAD

Serves: **2**

Prep Time: **5** Minutes

Cook Time: **5** Minutes

Total Time: **10** Minutes

INGREDIENTS

- 1 cup cooked lentils
- 1 tsp salt
- 1 cup cooked quinoa
- 2 tablespoons olive oil
- 1 tsp salt
- 1 tomato
- 1 avocado
- 1 tsp cilantro

DIRECTIONS

1. In a bowl mix all ingredients and mix well
2. Serve with dressing

CRANBERRY & SPINACH SALAD

Serves: **2**

Prep Time: **5** Minutes

Cook Time: **5** Minutes

Total Time: **10** Minutes

INGREDIENTS

- 2 cups cooked quinoa
- 1 cup spinach leaves
- ¼ cup cranberries
- ¼ cup walnuts
- ½ avocado

DIRECTIONS

1. In a bowl mix all ingredients and mix well
2. Serve with dressing

KALE SALAD

Serves: **2**

Prep Time: **5** Minutes

Cook Time: **5** Minutes

Total Time: **10** Minutes

INGREDIENTS

- 1 bunch kale
- 1 cup cooked chickpeas
- ¼ red onion
- ¼ cup tahini
- ¼ cup lemon juice
- 1 cup salad dressing

DIRECTIONS

1. **In a bowl mix all ingredients and mix well**
2. **Serve with dressing**

TORTELLINI SALAD

Serves: **2**

Prep Time: **5** Minutes

Cook Time: **5** Minutes

Total Time: **10** Minutes

INGREDIENTS

- 1 lb. tortellini
- ¼ cup olive oil
- 1 tablespoon balsamic vinegar
- 1 tsp salt
- 1 cup spinach leaves
- ½ cup Parmesan
- 1 cup tomatoes

DIRECTIONS

1. In a bowl mix all ingredients and mix well
2. Serve with dressing

TACO SALAD

Serves: 2

Prep Time: 5 Minutes

Cook Time: 5 Minutes

Total Time: 10 Minutes

INGREDIENTS

- ½ cup olive oil
- 1 lb. cooked steak
- 1 tablespoon taco seasoning
- Juice of 1 lime
- 1 tsp cumin
- 1 head romaine lettuce
- 1 cup corn
- 1 cup beans
- 1 cup tomatoes

DIRECTIONS

1. In a bowl mix all ingredients and mix well
2. Serve with dressing

DORITO TACO SALAD

Serves: 2
Prep Time: 5 Minutes
Cook Time: 5 Minutes
Total Time: 10 Minutes

INGREDIENTS

- 1 lb. cooked beef
- 1 tsp chili powder
- 1 tsp paprika
- 1 tsp cumin
- 1 head romaine lettuce
- 1 cup cherry tomatoes
- 1 cup cheddar cheese
- 1 avocado
- 1 bag doritos
- ¼ cup sour cream

DIRECTIONS

1. In a bowl mix all ingredients and mix well
2. Serve with dressing

CHEESEBURGER SALAD

Serves: **2**

Prep Time: **5** Minutes

Cook Time: **5** Minutes

Total Time: **10** Minutes

INGREDIENTS

- 1 lb. cooked beef
- 1 tsp garlic powder
- 1 tsp Worcestershire sauce
- 1 tsp black pepper
- 1 cup salad dressing
- 1 head romaine lettuce
- 1 cup cheddar cheese
- 1/4 red onion
- 1 tsp sesame seeds

DIRECTIONS

1. **In a bowl mix all ingredients and mix well**
2. **Serve with dressing**

MANDARIN SALAD

Serves: *2*

Prep Time: *5* Minutes

Cook Time: *5* Minutes

Total Time: *10* Minutes

INGREDIENTS

- 2 cups lettuce
- 2 cups red cabbage
- 2 cups cooked chicken
- ¼ cup carrot
- ¼ cup almonds

DRESSING

- 1 tablespoon honey
- 2 tablespoons rice wine vinegar
- 1 tablespoon soy sauce
- 1 tablespoon hoisin sauce

DIRECTIONS

1. In a bowl mix all ingredients and mix well
2. Serve with dressing

SOUTHWESTERN SALAD

Serves: **2**

Prep Time: **5** Minutes

Cook Time: **5** Minutes

Total Time: **10** Minutes

INGREDIENTS

- 1 lb. cooked penne
- 1 can corn kernels
- 1 can beans
- 1 cup cheddar cheese
- 1 avocado
- ½ cup cilantro
- 1 cup salad dressing

DIRECTIONS

1. **In a bowl mix all ingredients and mix well**
2. **Serve with dressing**

STEW RECIPES

BUTTERNUT SQUASH STEW

Serves: **4**

Prep Time: **15** Minutes

Cook Time: **45** Minutes

Total Time: **60** Minutes

INGREDIENTS

- 2 tablespoons olive oil
- 2 red onions
- 2 cloves garlic
- 1. Tablespoon rosemary
- 1 tablespoon thyme
- 2 lb. beef
- 1 cup white wine
- 1 cup butternut squash
- 2 cups beef broth
- ½ cup tomatoes

DIRECTIONS

1. Chop all ingredients in big chunks
2. In a large pot heat olive oil and add ingredients one by one
3. Cook for 5-6 or until slightly brown

4. Add remaining ingredients and cook until tender, 35-45 minutes
5. Season while stirring on low heat
6. When ready remove from heat and serve

BEEF STEW

Serves: *4*

Prep Time: *15* Minutes

Cook Time: *45* Minutes

Total Time: *60* Minutes

INGREDIENTS

- 2 lb. beef
- 1 tsp salt
- 4 tablespoons olive oil
- 2 red onions
- 2 cloves garlic
- 1 cup white wine
- 2 cups beef broth
- 1 cup water
- 3-4 bay leaves
- ¼ tsp thyme
- 1 lb. potatoes

DIRECTIONS

1. Chop all ingredients in big chunks
2. In a large pot heat olive oil and add ingredients one by one
3. Cook for 5-6 or until slightly brown

4. Add remaining ingredients and cook until tender, 35-45 minutes
5. Season while stirring on low heat
6. When ready remove from heat and serve

CASSEROLE RECIPES

CORN CASSEROLE

Serves: **4**

Prep Time: **10** Minutes

Cook Time: **15** Minutes

Total Time: **25** Minutes

INGREDIENTS

- ½ cup cornmeal
- ½ cup butter
- 2 eggs
- 1 cup milk
- ½ cup heavy cream
- 3 cups corn
- ¼ tsp smoked paprika

DIRECTIONS

1. Sauté the veggies and set aside
2. Preheat the oven to 425 F
3. Transfer the sautéed veggies to a baking dish, add remaining ingredients to the baking dish
4. Mix well, add seasoning and place the dish in the oven
5. Bake for 12-15 minutes or until slightly brown

6. When ready remove from the oven and serve

ARTICHOKE CASSEROLE

Serves: **4**

Prep Time: **10** Minutes

Cook Time: **15** Minutes

Total Time: **25** Minutes

INGREDIENTS

- 1 cup cooked rice
- 1 cup milk
- 1 cup parmesan cheese
- 4 oz. cream cheese
- 1 lb. cooked chicken breast
- 1 cup spinach
- 1 can artichoke hearts
- 1 cup mozzarella cheese

DIRECTIONS

1. Sauté the veggies and set aside
2. Preheat the oven to 425 F
3. Transfer the sautéed veggies to a baking dish, add remaining ingredients to the baking dish
4. Mix well, add seasoning and place the dish in the oven
5. Bake for 12-15 minutes or until slightly brown
6. When ready remove from the oven and serve

PIZZA RECIPES

MUSHROOM PIZZA

Serves: **2**

Prep Time: **10** Minutes

Cook Time: **30** Minutes

Total Time: **40** Minutes

INGREDIENTS

- 2 button mushrooms
- ½ red onion
- 1 lemon juiced
- 1 tablespoon parsley
- ½ cup ground flax seeds
- 2 tablespoons olive oil
- 1 cup almonds whole
- 1 cup cashews whole
- 1 carrot

DIRECTIONS

1. Preheat oven to 375 F and place a baking sheet
2. In food processor place all the ingredients and blend for 8-10 minutes

3. Pour the mixture on the baking sheet and bake for 15-20 minutes until golden
4. Remove from the oven and serve

CASSEROLE PIZZA

Serves: **6-8**

Prep Time: **10** Minutes

Cook Time: **15** Minutes

Total Time: **25** Minutes

INGREDIENTS

- 1 pizza crust
- ½ cup tomato sauce
- ¼ black pepper
- 1 cup zucchini slices
- 1 cup mozzarella cheese
- 1 cup olives

DIRECTIONS

1. Spread tomato sauce on the pizza crust
2. Place all the toppings on the pizza crust
3. Bake the pizza at 425 F for 12-15 minutes
4. When ready remove pizza from the oven and serve

SECOND COOKBOOK

BREAKFAST RECIPES

MUSHROOM OMELETTE

Serves: *1*

Prep Time: *5* Minutes

Cook Time: *5* Minutes

Total Time: *10* Minutes

INGREDIENTS

- 2 eggs
- Bacon
- 2 tsp coconut oil
- Nutmeg
- 1 red onion
- Salt
- Pepper

DIRECTIONS

1. Sauté the onion in the coconut oil for a few minutes.
2. Slice the mushrooms and add them to the pan, with salt and nutmeg.
3. Cook for another few minutes.
4. Remove the mushrooms from the pan.
5. Cook the beaten eggs for 3 minutes.

6. Serve the omelette topped with the mushroom mixture and bacon.

AVOCADO TOAST

Serves: **1**

Prep Time: **5** Minutes

Cook Time: **10** Minutes

Total Time: **15** Minutes

INGREDIENTS

- 1 clove garlic
- ½ avocado
- 1 egg
- Salt
- 1 slice toast
- Pepper
- Red pepper flakes

DIRECTIONS

1. Grate ½ clove of garlic into a pan, add the egg on top and cook to the desired degree of doneness.
2. Toast the bread.
3. Smash the avocado with a fork.
4. Spread the avocado over the toast.
5. Top with the fried egg and garlic, season, and serve.

TOMATO SHAKSHUKA

Serves: **4**

Prep Time: **10** Minutes

Cook Time: **50** Minutes

Total Time: **60** Minutes

INGREDIENTS

- 1 pinch cayenne
- Salt
- 1 red bell pepper
- 4 eggs
- ¼ cup olive oil
- 1 tbs cumin seeds
- 1 yellow onion
- 2 thyme sprigs
- 1 tbs parsley
- 1 ½ lb cherry tomatoes

DIRECTIONS

1. Preheat the oven to 350F.
2. Cut the tomatoes and place them on a cookie sheet, then season with salt.
3. Bake until fully roasted.
4. Roast the cumin seeds for 1 minute.

5. Add the olive oil and onion and saute until soft.
6. Add the strips chopped pepper, chopped herbs, and tomatoes.
7. Add the salt and cayenne pepper.
8. Pour the eggs into the pan and cook on low until the egg white is set.
9. Serve immediately.

PORTOBELLO MUSHROOM CAPS

Serves: *1*
Prep Time: *5* Minutes
Cook Time: *5* Minutes
Total Time: *10* Minutes

INGREDIENTS

- 50g ham
- Salt
- Pepper
- ¼ cup watercress
- 1 Portobello mushroom
- 1 poached egg
- ½ avocado

DIRECTIONS

1. Cook the mushrooms in coconut oil for 1 minute per side.
2. Season with salt and set aside.
3. Poach the eggs.
4. Pot each Portobello cap with the sliced avocado, a handful of watercress leaves, and ham.
5. Place the egg over, sprinkle with salt and pepper and serve.

EGG IN AVOCADO

Serves: 2
Prep Time: 5 Minutes
Cook Time: 10 Minutes
Total Time: 15 Minutes

INGREDIENTS

- 1 avocado
- 2 eggs
- Cheese
- Salt
- Pepper

DIRECTIONS

1. Preheat the oven to 425F.
2. Slice the avocado in half and remove the pit.
3. Crave out a little space in the center and crack the egg there.
4. Top with cheese.
5. Cook until the cheese is melted and the egg is done.
6. Serve immediately.

OMELETTE BITES

Serves: **12**

Prep Time: **5** Minutes

Cook Time: **35** Minutes

Total Time: **40** Minutes

INGREDIENTS

- 4 eggs
- 1 green pepper
- 2 cups diced cooked chicken
- 2 cups spinach
- 1 avocado
- 12 egg whites
- Pepper
- 12 slices bacon
- 1 red pepper

DIRECTIONS

1. Preheat the oven to 350F.
2. Cook the bacon for 5 minutes, making sure it's not crispy.
3. Grease a muffin tin and place one piece of bacon in each tin, wrapping it around the outer edges.
4. Whisk together in a bowl the eggs, egg whites, salt, pepper, peppers, chicken, and spinach.

5. Mix well then pour into each muffin tin.
6. Bake for 30 minutes, serve topped with avocado.

MACADAMIA WAFFLES

Serves: **6**

Prep Time: **10** Minutes

Cook Time: **3** Minutes

Total Time: **40** Minutes

INGREDIENTS

- 4 tbs coconut flour
- 1 cup macadamia nuts
- ½ cup coconut milk
- 1 tsp baking powder
- 3 eggs
- 1 tsp vanilla
- 3 tbs maple syrup
- 3 tbs coconut oil

DIRECTIONS

1. Preheat the waffle iron.
2. Blend all of the ingredients for 30 seconds on low.
3. Blend on high for another 30 seconds, until completely smooth.
4. Pour the batter into the waffle iron.
5. Cook on low for 50 seconds.
6. Serve topped with your desired syrups.

BACON & AVOCADO SANDWICHES

Serves: 2
Prep Time: 5 Minutes
Cook Time: 5 Minutes
Total Time: *10* Minutes

INGREDIENTS

- Salt
- 1 avocado
- 4 strips bacon
- 1 lime

DIRECTIONS

1. Cook the bacon.
2. Mash the avocado with lime juice and salt.
3. Place the avocado mixture between the bacon slices.
4. Serve immediately.

ZUCCHINI FRITTATA

Serves: **4**

Prep Time: **10** Minutes

Cook Time: **25** Minutes

Total Time: **35** Minutes

INGREDIENTS

- 1 sweet potato
- 2 zucchinis
- 8 eggs
- 1 red bell pepper
- 2 tbs coconut oil
- 2 tbs parsley
- Salt
- Pepper

DIRECTIONS

1. Cook the potato slices in the oil for 10 minutes.
2. Add the zucchini and bell peppers and cook for another 5 minutes.
3. Whisk the eggs in a bowl.
4. Season with salt and pepper and add it to the veggies.
5. Cook on low for 10 minutes.
6. Serve topped with fresh parsley.

SWEET POTATO BREAKFAST CAKE

Serves: **4**

Prep Time: **30** Minutes

Cook Time: **15** Minutes

Total Time: **35** Minutes

INGREDIENTS

- 2 tbs oil
- 2 tbs parsley
- 1 red onion
- 3 egg whites
- 2 sweet potatoes
- ½ cup dried cranberries
- 6 eggs
- Salt
- Pepper

DIRECTIONS

1. **Preheat the oven to 425F.**
2. **Poke holes all around the potatoes using a fork.**
3. **Add the cranberries, parsley, onion, salt, and pepper.**
4. **Add 2 whisked egg whites.**
5. **Make patties from the mixture.**
6. **Cook in oil for 4 minutes on each side.**

7. Place the cooked patties onto a greased baking dish.
8. Push down in the middle of each patty, creating space for the eggs.
9. Crack the eggs on top, into the created space.
10. Bake for 15 minutes.
11. Caramelize the onion in a skillet.
12. Serve topped with the caramelized onions.

MINI EGG OMELETS

Serves: **4**

Prep Time: **10** Minutes

Cook Time: **20** Minutes

Total Time: **30** Minutes

INGREDIENTS

- ¼ cup shredded cheddar
- 4 eggs
- ¼ cup cheese
- 1 ½ tsp olive oil
- 4 cups broccoli florets
- Salt
- Pepper
- 1 cup egg whites

DIRECTIONS

1. Preheat the oven to 350F.
2. Steam the broccoli for 5 minutes.
3. Once cooked, crumble into smaller pieces and add olive oil, salt, and pepper.
4. Grease a muffin tin and pour the mixture into each tin.
5. Beat the egg whites, eggs, cheese, salt and pepper in a bowl.
6. Pour over the broccoli, top with cheese and cook for 20 minutes.

BREAKFAST MEATCAKES

Serves: **14**

Prep Time: **10** Minutes

Cook Time: **40** Minutes

Total Time: **50** Minutes

INGREDIENTS

- 1 lb pork sausage
- 6 ounces blackberries
- 1 tsp cinnamon
- 1 ½ tsp salt
- 1 tsp black pepper
- 1 tsp rosemary
- 1 tsp thyme
- 1 orange zest
- 1 ln chicken breast
- 12 strips bacon
- 1 apple
- 1 tsp garlic powder

DIRECTIONS

1. Preheat the oven to 375F.
2. Dice the apple.
3. Line the cupcake pans with bacon.

4. Mix together, smashing with hands, sausage, spices, chicken, apple, zest, and blackberries.
5. Fill the pan with the mixture.
6. Bake for 35 minutes.
7. Serve topped with zest or blackberries.

CANTALOUPE PANCAKES

Serves: **4**

Prep Time: **10** Minutes

Cook Time: **20** Minutes

Total Time: **30** Minutes

INGREDIENTS

- 1 cup whole wheat flour
- ¼ tsp baking soda
- ¼ tsp baking powder
- 2 eggs
- 1 cup milk
- 1 cup cantaloupe

DIRECTIONS

1. In a bowl combine all ingredients together and mix well
2. In a skillet heat olive oil
3. Pour ¼ of the batter and cook each pancake for 1-2 minutes per side
4. When ready remove from heat and serve

COCONUT PANCAKES

Serves: **4**

Prep Time: **10** Minutes

Cook Time: **20** Minutes

Total Time: **30** Minutes

INGREDIENTS

- 1 cup whole wheat flour
- ¼ tsp baking soda
- ¼ tsp baking powder
- 1 cup coconut flalkes
- 2 eggs
- 1 cup milk

DIRECTIONS

1. In a bowl combine all ingredients together and mix well
2. In a skillet heat olive oil
3. Pour ¼ of the batter and cook each pancake for 1-2 minutes per side
4. When ready remove from heat and serve

CHERRIES PANCAKES

Serves: **4**

Prep Time: **10** Minutes

Cook Time: **30** Minutes

Total Time: **40** Minutes

INGREDIENTS

- 1 cup whole wheat flour
- ¼ tsp baking soda
- ¼ tsp baking powder
- 2 eggs
- 1 cup milk
- 1 cup cherries

DIRECTIONS

1. In a bowl combine all ingredients together and mix well
2. In a skillet heat olive oil
3. Pour ¼ of the batter and cook each pancake for 1-2 minutes per side
4. When ready remove from heat and serve

MANGO MUFFINS

Serves: **8-12**

Prep Time: **10** Minutes

Cook Time: **20** Minutes

Total Time: **30** Minutes

INGREDIENTS

- 2 eggs
- 1 tablespoon olive oil
- 1 cup milk
- 2 cups whole wheat flour
- 1 tsp baking soda
- ¼ tsp baking soda
- 1 tsp ginger
- 1 tsp cinnamon
- 1 cup mango

DIRECTIONS

1. In a bowl combine all wet ingredients
2. In another bowl combine all dry ingredients
3. Combine wet and dry ingredients together
4. Pour mixture into 8-12 prepared muffin cups, fill 2/3 of the cups
5. Bake for 18-20 minutes at 375 F, when ready remove and serve

NECTARINE MUFFINS

Serves: *8-12*

Prep Time: *10* Minutes

Cook Time: *20* Minutes

Total Time: *30* Minutes

INGREDIENTS

- 2 eggs
- 1 tablespoon olive oil
- 1 cup milk
- 2 cups whole wheat flour
- 1 tsp baking soda
- ¼ tsp baking soda
- 1 tsp cinnamon
- 1 cup nectarine

DIRECTIONS

1. In a bowl combine all wet ingredients
2. In another bowl combine all dry ingredients
3. Combine wet and dry ingredients together
4. Pour mixture into 8-12 prepared muffin cups, fill 2/3 of the cups
5. Bake for 18-20 minutes at 375 F
6. When ready remove from the oven and serve

PAPAYA MUFFINS

Serves: **8-12**
Prep Time: **10** Minutes
Cook Time: **20** Minutes
Total Time: **30** Minutes

INGREDIENTS

- 2 eggs
- 1 tablespoon olive oil
- 1 cup milk
- 2 cups whole wheat flour
- 1 tsp baking soda
- ¼ tsp baking soda
- 1 tsp cinnamon
- 1 cup papaya

DIRECTIONS

1. In a bowl combine all wet ingredients
2. In another bowl combine all dry ingredients
3. Combine wet and dry ingredients together
4. Pour mixture into 8-12 prepared muffin cups, fill 2/3 of the cups
5. Bake for 18-20 minutes at 375 F
6. When ready remove from the oven and serve

PLANTAIN MUFFINS

Serves: *8-12*

Prep Time: *10* Minutes

Cook Time: *20* Minutes

Total Time: *30* Minutes

INGREDIENTS

- 2 eggs
- 1 tablespoon olive oil
- 1 cup milk
- 2 cups whole wheat flour
- 1 tsp baking soda
- ¼ tsp baking soda
- 1 tsp cinnamon
- 1 cup plantain

DIRECTIONS

1. In a bowl combine all wet ingredients
2. In another bowl combine all dry ingredients
3. Combine wet and dry ingredients together
4. Pour mixture into 8-12 prepared muffin cups, fill 2/3 of the cups
5. Bake for 18-20 minutes at 375 F
6. When ready remove from the oven and serve

ONION OMELETTE

Serves: **1**

Prep Time: **5** Minutes

Cook Time: **10** Minutes

Total Time: **15** Minutes

INGREDIENTS

- 2 eggs
- ¼ tsp salt
- ¼ tsp black pepper
- 1 tablespoon olive oil
- ¼ cup cheese
- ¼ tsp basil
- 1 cup red onion

DIRECTIONS

1. In a bowl combine all ingredients together and mix well
2. In a skillet heat olive oil and pour the egg mixture
3. Cook for 1-2 minutes per side
4. When ready remove omelette from the skillet and serve

BEETROOT OMELETTE

Serves: **1**

Prep Time: **5** Minutes

Cook Time: **10** Minutes

Total Time: **15** Minutes

INGREDIENTS

- 2 eggs
- ¼ tsp salt
- ¼ tsp black pepper
- 1 tablespoon olive oil
- ¼ cup cheese
- ¼ tsp basil
- 1 cup mushrooms

DIRECTIONS

1. In a bowl combine all ingredients together and mix well
2. In a skillet heat olive oil and pour the egg mixture
3. Cook for 1-2 minutes per side
4. When ready remove omelette from the skillet and serve

BELL PEPPER OMELETTE

Serves: *1*

Prep Time: *5* Minutes

Cook Time: *10* Minutes

Total Time: *15* Minutes

INGREDIENTS

- 2 eggs
- ¼ tsp salt
- ¼ tsp black pepper
- 1 tablespoon olive oil
- ¼ cup cheese
- ¼ tsp basil
- 1 cup yellow bell pepper

DIRECTIONS

1. In a bowl combine all ingredients together and mix well
2. In a skillet heat olive oil and pour the egg mixture
3. Cook for 1-2 minutes per side
4. When ready remove omelette from the skillet and serve

TART RECIPES

PEAR TART

Serves: **6-8**

Prep Time: 25 Minutes

Cook Time: 25 Minutes

Total Time: 50 Minutes

INGREDIENTS

- 1 lb. pears
- 2 oz. brown sugar
- ½ lb. flaked almonds
- ¼ lb. porridge oat
- 2 oz. flour
- ¼ lb. almonds
- pastry sheets
- 2 tablespoons syrup

DIRECTIONS

1. Preheat oven to 400 F, unfold pastry sheets and place them on a baking sheet
2. Toss together all ingredients together and mix well

3. Spread mixture in a single layer on the pastry sheets
4. Before baking decorate with your desired fruits
5. Bake at 400 F for 22-25 minutes or until golden brown
6. When ready remove from the oven and serve

CARDAMOM TART

Serves: **6-8**

Prep Time: **25** Minutes

Cook Time: **25** Minutes

Total Time: **50** Minutes

INGREDIENTS

- 4-5 pears
- 2 tablespoons lemon juice
- pastry sheets

CARDAMOM FILLING

- ½ lb. butter
- ½ lb. brown sugar
- ½ lb. almonds
- ¼ lb. flour
- 1 ¼ tsp cardamom
- 2 eggs

DIRECTIONS

1. Preheat oven to 400 F, unfold pastry sheets and place them on a baking sheet
2. Toss together all ingredients together and mix well
3. Spread mixture in a single layer on the pastry sheets
4. Before baking decorate with your desired fruits

5. Bake at 400 F for 22-25 minutes or until golden brown
6. When ready remove from the oven and serve

PIE RECIPES

PEACH PECAN PIE

Serves: **8-12**

Prep Time: **15** Minutes
Cook Time: **35** Minutes
Total Time: **50** Minutes

INGREDIENTS

- 4-5 cups peaches
- 1 tablespoon preserves
- 1 cup sugar
- 4 small egg yolks
- ¼ cup flour
- 1 tsp vanilla extract

DIRECTIONS

1. Line a pie plate or pie form with pastry and cover the edges of the plate depending on your preference
2. In a bowl combine all pie ingredients together and mix well
3. Pour the mixture over the pastry
4. Bake at 400-425 F for 25-30 minutes or until golden brown
5. When ready remove from the oven and let it rest for 15 minutes

BUTTERFINGER PIE

Serves: *8-12*

Prep Time: *15* Minutes

Cook Time: *35* Minutes

Total Time: *50* Minutes

INGREDIENTS

- pastry sheets
- 1 package cream cheese
- 1 tsp vanilla extract
- ¼ cup peanut butter
- 1 cup powdered sugar (to decorate)
- 2 cups Butterfinger candy bars
- 8 oz whipped topping

DIRECTIONS

1. Line a pie plate or pie form with pastry and cover the edges of the plate depending on your preference
2. In a bowl combine all pie ingredients together and mix well
3. Pour the mixture over the pastry
4. Bake at 400-425 F for 25-30 minutes or until golden brown
5. When ready remove from the oven and let it rest for 15 minutes

STRAWBERRY PIE

Serves: *8-12*

Prep Time: *15* Minutes

Cook Time: *35* Minutes

Total Time: *50* Minutes

INGREDIENTS

- pastry sheets
- 1,5 lb. strawberries
- 1 cup powdered sugar
- 2 tablespoons cornstarch
- 1 tablespoon lime juice
- 1 tsp vanilla extract
- 2 eggs
- 2 tablespoons butter

DIRECTIONS

1. Line a pie plate or pie form with pastry and cover the edges of the plate depending on your preference
2. In a bowl combine all pie ingredients together and mix well
3. Pour the mixture over the pastry
4. Bake at 400-425 F for 25-30 minutes or until golden brown
5. When ready remove from the oven and let it rest for 15 minutes

BLUEBERRY PIE

Serves: **8-12**

Prep Time: **15** Minutes

Cook Time: **35** Minutes

Total Time: **50** Minutes

INGREDIENTS

- pastry sheets
- ¼ tsp lavender
- 1 cup brown sugar
- 4-5 cups blueberries
- 1 tablespoon lemon juice
- 1 cup almonds
- 2 tablespoons butter

DIRECTIONS

1. Line a pie plate or pie form with pastry and cover the edges of the plate depending on your preference
2. In a bowl combine all pie ingredients together and mix well
3. Pour the mixture over the pastry
4. Bake at 400-425 F for 25-30 minutes or until golden brown
5. When ready remove from the oven and let it rest for 15 minutes

SMOOTHIE RECIPES

GINGER-OAT SMOOTHIE

Serves: **1**

Prep Time: **5** Minutes

Cook Time: **5** Minutes

Total Time: **10** Minutes

INGREDIENTS

- ½ cup oats
- ¼ cup blueberries
- ¼ cup vanilla yogurt
- 1 cup ice
- ¼ tsp ginger

DIRECTIONS

1. In a blender place all ingredients and blend until smooth
2. Pour smoothie in a glass and serve

PUMPKIN SMOOTHIE

Serves: **1**

Prep Time: **5** Minutes

Cook Time: **5** Minutes

Total Time: **10** Minutes

INGREDIENTS

- 1 cup ice
- 1 cup almond milk
- ½ cup pumpkin puree
- 1 tsp honey

DIRECTIONS

1. **In a blender place all ingredients and blend until smooth**
2. **Pour smoothie in a glass and serve**

GREEN SMOOTHIE

Serves: *1*

Prep Time: *5* Minutes

Cook Time: *5* Minutes

Total Time: *10* Minutes

INGREDIENTS

- 1 cup kale
- 1 celery
- 1 banana
- 1 cup apple juice
- 1 cup ice

DIRECTIONS

1. **In a blender place all ingredients and blend until smooth**
2. **Pour smoothie in a glass and serve**

MANGO SMOOTHIE

Serves: **1**

Prep Time: **5** Minutes

Cook Time: **5** Minutes

Total Time: **10** Minutes

INGREDIENTS

- 1 cup mango
- ½ cup coconut milk
- 1 cup ice
- ½ cup vanilla yogurt
- 1 tsp honey

DIRECTIONS

1. **In a blender place all ingredients and blend until smooth**
2. **Pour smoothie in a glass and serve**

PINEAPPLE SMOOTHIE

Serves: *1*

Prep Time: *5* Minutes

Cook Time: *5* Minutes

Total Time: *10* Minutes

INGREDIENTS

- 1 cup pineapple
- 1 cup ice
- 1 orange juice
- ½ cup carrot
- 1 banana

DIRECTIONS

1. In a blender place all ingredients and blend until smooth
2. Pour smoothie in a glass and serve

CASHEW SMOOTHIE

Serves: **1**
Prep Time: **5** Minutes
Cook Time: **5** Minutes
Total Time: **10** Minutes

INGREDIENTS

- 1 cup cashews
- 1 cup ice
- 1 banana
- 1 tablespoon honey

DIRECTIONS

1. In a blender place all ingredients and blend until smooth
2. Pour smoothie in a glass and serve

NUT SMOOTHIE

Serves: *1*

Prep Time: *5* Minutes

Cook Time: *5* Minutes

Total Time: *10* Minutes

INGREDIENTS

- 1 cup coconut milk
- 1 cup raspberries
- 1 banana
- 1 tablespoon peanut butter
- 1 tsp agave nectar

DIRECTIONS

1. **In a blender place all ingredients and blend until smooth**
2. **Pour smoothie in a glass and serve**

STRAWBERRY SMOOTHIE

Serves: **1**
Prep Time: **5** Minutes
Cook Time: **5** Minutes
Total Time: **10** Minutes

INGREDIENTS

- 1 cup strawberries
- 1 cup Greek Yoghurt
- ½ cup orange juice
- 1 tsp honey
- 1 tablespoon flaxseed meal

DIRECTIONS

1. In a blender place all ingredients and blend until smooth
2. Pour smoothie in a glass and serve

SPINACH & GRAPE SMOOTHIE

Serves: *1*
Prep Time: *5* Minutes
Cook Time: *5* Minutes
Total Time: *10* Minutes

INGREDIENTS

- 1 cup grapes
- 1 cup baby spinach
- 1 cup ice
- 1 cup almond milk

DIRECTIONS

1. **In a blender place all ingredients and blend until smooth**
2. **Pour smoothie in a glass and serve**

ICE-CREAM RECIPES

SAFFRON ICE-CREAM

Serves: **6-8**

Prep Time: **15** Minutes
Cook Time: **15** Minutes
Total Time: **30** Minutes

INGREDIENTS

- 4 egg yolks
- 1 cup heavy cream
- 1 cup milk
- ½ cup brown sugar
- 1 tsp saffron
- 1 tsp vanilla extract

DIRECTIONS

1. In a saucepan whisk together all ingredients
2. Mix until bubbly
3. Strain into a bowl and cool
4. Whisk in favorite fruits and mix well
5. Cover and refrigerate for 2-3 hours

6. Pour mixture in the ice-cream maker and follow manufacturer instructions
7. Serve when ready

PISTACHIOS ICE-CREAM

Serves: **6-8**

Prep Time: **15** Minutes
Cook Time: **15** Minutes
Total Time: **30** Minutes

INGREDIENTS

- 4 egg yolks
- 1 cup heavy cream
- 1 cup milk
- 1 cup sugar
- 1 vanilla bean
- 1 tsp almond extract
- 1 cup cherries
- ½ cup pistachios

DIRECTIONS

1. In a saucepan whisk together all ingredients
2. Mix until bubbly
3. Strain into a bowl and cool
4. Whisk in favorite fruits and mix well
5. Cover and refrigerate for 2-3 hours
6. Pour mixture in the ice-cream maker and follow manufacturer instructions

VANILLA ICE-CREAM

Serves: **6-8**

Prep Time: **15** Minutes
Cook Time: **15** Minutes
Total Time: **30** Minutes

INGREDIENTS

- 1 cup milk
- 1 tablespoon cornstarch
- 1 oz. cream cheese
- 1 cup heavy cream
- 1 cup brown sugar
- 1 tablespoon corn syrup
- 1 vanilla bean

DIRECTIONS

1. In a saucepan whisk together all ingredients
2. Mix until bubbly
3. Strain into a bowl and cool
4. Whisk in favorite fruits and mix well
5. Cover and refrigerate for 2-3 hours
6. Pour mixture in the ice-cream maker and follow manufacturer instructions
7. Serve when ready

THIRD COOKBOOK

SOUP RECIPES

ZUCCHINI SOUP

Serves: **4**

Prep Time: **10** Minutes

Cook Time: **20** Minutes

Total Time: **30** Minutes

INGREDIENTS

- 1 tablespoon olive oil
- 1 lb. zucchini
- ¼ red onion
- ½ cup all-purpose flour
- ¼ tsp salt
- ¼ tsp pepper
- 1 can vegetable broth
- 1 cup heavy cream

DIRECTIONS

1. In a saucepan heat olive oil and sauté zucchini until tender
2. Add remaining ingredients to the saucepan and bring to a boil
3. When all the vegetables are tender transfer to a blender and blend until smooth
4. Pour soup into bowls, garnish with parsley and serve

BROCCOLI SOUP

Serves: **2**

Prep Time: **10** Minutes

Cook Time: **10** Minutes

Total Time: **20** Minutes

INGREDIENTS

- 1 onion
- 2 cloves garlic
- 1 tbs butter
- 2 cup broccoli
- 1 potato
- 3 cup chicken broth
- 1 cup cheddar cheese
- 1/3 cup buttermilk
- Salt
- Pepper

DIRECTIONS

1. Cook the onion and garlic in melted butter for 5 minutes
2. Add the diced potato, broccoli florets and chicken broth
3. Bring to a boil, then reduce the heat and simmer for at least 5 minutes
4. Allow to cool, then pulse until smooth using a blender

5. Return to the saucepan and add the buttermilk and ¼ cup cheese
6. Cook for about 3 minutes
7. Season with salt and pepper
8. Serve topped with the remaining cheese

CHICKEN NOODLE SOUP

Serves: **6**

Prep Time: **40** Minutes

Cook Time: **80** Minutes

Total Time: **120** Minutes

INGREDIENTS

Broth:
- 15 peppercorns
- 2 onions
- 2 carrots
- 1 rib celery
- 3 sprigs thyme
- 5 cloves garlic
- 3 bay leaves
- 8 chicken thighs

Soup:
- 2 chicken bouillon cubes
- 1 tsp salt
- 5 oz egg noodles
- 1/3 cup parsley
- 2 ribs celery
- 2 carrots

DIRECTIONS

1. Place the broth ingredients in a pot with 12 cups of water
2. Bring to a boil, then reduce the heat and simmer for about 20 minutes
3. Remove the chicken and shred meat from bones
4. Return the bones to the pot and continue to simmer for another 60 minutes
5. Strain the broth and discard the bones and other solids
6. Skim broth and bring to a boil
7. Add the soup ingredients except for the parsley
8. Stir in the noodles and cook for at least 5 minutes
9. Stir in the chicken meat and parsley and cook 1 more minute
10. Serve immediately

TORTILLA SOUP

Serves: **6**

Prep Time: **10** Minutes

Cook Time: **10** Minutes

Total Time: **20** Minutes

INGREDIENTS

- 1/3 cup rice
- 15 oz salsa
- 1 can black beans
- 30 oz chicken broth
- 1 cup corn
- Chicken

DIRECTIONS

1. Place the broth and the salsa in a pot and bring to a boil
2. Add rice, beans and cooked chicken
3. Simmer covered for about 10 minutes
4. Stir in the corn
5. Serve topped with cheese

ASPARAGUS SOUP

Serves: *4*

Prep Time: *15* Minutes

Cook Time: *35* Minutes

Total Time: *50* Minutes

INGREDIENTS

- 2 tbs oil
- 1/3 tsp salt
- 1 cup bread cubes
- 1 cup potato
- 2 tsp horseradish
- 3 cups chicken broth
- 1 lb asparagus
- Scallions
- 1 shallot

DIRECTIONS

1. Cook the shallot until soft for 2 minutes
2. Add the asparagus, potato, broth, horseradish and salt and bring to a boil
3. Reduce the heat and simmer for about 15 minutes
4. Pulse using a blender
5. Cook the bread cubes in hot oil until crispy, serve with croutons

LENTIL SOUP

Serves: **9**

Prep Time: **10** Minutes

Cook Time: **50** Minutes

Total Time: **60** Minutes

INGREDIENTS

- 2 tbs oil
- 1 stalk celery
- 1 red bell pepper
- 2 cans chicken broth
- 1 onion
- 1 cup carrots
- 2 garlic cloves
- 2 tsp cumin
- 1 tsp coriander
- 1 can tomatoes
- 2 sweet potatoes
- 3 tsp thyme leaves
- 2 cups red lentils

DIRECTIONS

1. Cook the onion, celery, carrots and red pepper in hot oil for 3 minutes

2. Add garlic, thyme, cumin and coriander and cook for 10 more minutes
3. Add the broth, sweet potatoes, lentils and tomatoes
4. Bring to a boil, then reduce the heat and simmer for at least 30 minutes
5. Pulse using a blender
6. Serve immediately

BROCCOLI AND RED CAPSICUM SOUP

Serves: **4**

Prep Time: **10** Minutes

Cook Time: **15** Minutes

Total Time: **25** Minutes

INGREDIENTS

- 1 cup broccoli florets
- 1 cup red capsicum
- 1 tsp oil
- 1 tablespoon garlic
- ¼ cup onions
- pinch of salt
- 1 tsp pepper powder

DIRECTIONS

1. In a pan sauté onions and garlic for 2-3 minutes
2. Add salt, red capsicum, broccoli, 1 cup water, and mix well
3. Cover with a lid cook for 5-6 minutes
4. When ready remove from heat and blend using a mixer
5. Transfer the mixture back to the pan, add ¼ cup water, pepper powder and cook for another 2-3 minutes
6. When ready remove from heat and serve

CANTALOUPE SOUP

Serves: **4**

Prep Time: **10** Minutes

Cook Time: **15** Minutes

Total Time: **25** Minutes

INGREDIENTS

- 2 cantaloupes
- 1 tsp ginger
- ½ tsp nutmeg
- ½ cup fat-free sour cream

DIRECTIONS

1. **Remove seeds from cantaloupes and refrigerate**
2. **Pour melon into a blender with spices, sour cream and blend until smooth**
3. **Refrigerate for another hour and pour soup into the bowl**
4. **Garnish with nutmeg, ginger and serve**

SIDE DISHES

GREEN PESTO PASTA

Serves: **2**

Prep Time: **5** Minutes

Cook Time: **15** Minutes

Total Time: **20** Minutes

INGREDIENTS

- 4 oz. spaghetti
- 2 cups basil leaves
- 2 garlic cloves
- ¼ cup olive oil
- 2 tablespoons parmesan cheese
- ½ tsp black pepper

DIRECTIONS

1. Bring water to a boil and add pasta
2. In a blend add parmesan cheese, basil leaves, garlic and blend
3. Add olive oil, pepper and blend again
4. Pour pesto onto pasta and serve when ready

BUCKWHEAT DOSA

Serves: **4**

Prep Time: **5** Minutes

Cook Time: **20** Minutes

Total Time: **25** Minutes

INGREDIENTS

- 1 cup buckwheat
- 1 tablespoon olive oil
- 1 tsp mustard seeds
- ½ tsp asafetida
- 1 tsp green chilies
- 1 tablespoon coriander
- 1 tablespoon urad dal

DIRECTIONS

1. In a bowl combine urad dal and buckwheat, using a mixer blend until smooth
2. In a pan add mustard seeds, asafetida, chilies, salt, coriander, water, and mix well
3. Pour 1/3 cup batter in a circular manner and cook until golden brown
4. When ready remove and serve

ZUCCHINI BAJRA KHICHDI

Serves: **3**

Prep Time: **10** Minutes

Cook Time: **30** Minutes

Total Time: **40** Minutes

INGREDIENTS

- ½ cup zucchini
- ¼ cup bajra
- 1 tsp olive oil
- 1 tsp cumin seeds
- ¼ cup red capsicum
- ¼ cup green capsicum
- ¼ cup almond milk
- ¼ tsp chili paste
- ¼ cup coriander

DIRECTIONS

1. Soak the bajra in water overnight
2. In a pressure cooker combine water, bajra and mix well
3. Allow the steam to go away before opening the lid
4. In a pan add cumin seeds, asafetida and sauté for 1-2 minutes
5. Add capsicum, zucchini, salt and sauté for another 3-4 minutes

6. Add milk, coriander, chili paste and cook for another 2-3 minutes
7. When ready remove from heat and serve

QUINOA MUTHIA

Serves: **5**

Prep Time: **10** Minutes

Cook Time: **40** Minutes

Total Time: **50** Minutes

INGREDIENTS

- ½ cup quinoa flour
- 1 cup besan
- ¼ cup semolina
- 1 cup bottle gourd
- 6 tsp oil
- 2 tsp chilli paste
- 1 pinch baking soda
- ¼ tsp asafetida
- ¼ tsp turmeric powder
- 1 tsp lemon juice
- 1 tsp mustard seeds
- 1 tsp sesame seeds
- 3 curry leaves
- 1 tablespoon coriander

DIRECTIONS

1. In a bowl combine semolina, besan, quinoa flour, 1 tsp oil, chili paste, gourd, asafetida, turmeric powder, lemon juice, and salt
2. Divide mixture into 4-5 portions and shape them into patties
3. Steam in a steamer for 10-15 minutes
4. When ready, remove from the steamer
5. In a pan add remaining oil, sesame seeds, curry leaves, asafetida and sauté for 1 minute
6. Add muthia, sauté for 2-3 minutes and serve with coriander

LIME GRILLED CORN

Serves: 3

Prep Time: 5 Minutes

Cook Time: 15 Minutes

Total Time: 20 Minutes

INGREDIENTS

- 3 ears of corn
- 2 tablespoons mayonnaise
- 2 tablespoons squeezed lime juice
- ½ tsp chili powder
- 1 pinch of salt

DIRECTIONS

1. Place corn onto the grill and cook for 5-6 minutes or until the kernels being to brown
2. Turn every few minutes until all sides are slightly charred
3. In a bowl mix the rest of ingredients
4. Spread a light coating of the mixture onto each corn and serve

CAPSICUM AND PANEER SUBZI

Serves: 5

Prep Time: 10 Minutes

Cook Time: 15 Minutes

Total Time: 25 Minutes

INGREDIENTS

- 2 cups capsicum cubes
- ¼ cup paneer
- 1 tsp oil
- ¼ cup onion cubes
- ¼ tsp ginger paste
- 1 tsp garlic paste
- 1 tsp dried fenugreek leaves
- 1 cup tomato pulp
- ¼ tsp turmeric powder
- ¼ tsp chili powder
- 1 tsp garam masala
- pinch of salt

DIRECTIONS

1. In a pan sauté onion
2. Add garlic paste, fenugreek leaves, ginger paste and sauté for 1 minute

3. Add capsicum, turmeric powder, tomato pulp, chili powder, garam masala and mix well
4. Cook for 5-6 minutes, add salt, paneer and mix well
5. Cook for another 2-3 minutes, when ready remove from heat and serve

AVOCADO DIP

Serves: **4**

Prep Time: **5** Minutes

Cook Time: **5** Minutes

Total Time: **10** Minutes

INGREDIENTS

- 1 cup mashed avocado
- 1 tsp lemon juice
- 1 tablespoon tomatoes
- ¼ tsp green chilies
- pinch of salt

DIRECTIONS

1. **In a bowl combine all ingredients together and mix well**
2. **When ready serve with corn chips**

ONION PURIS

Serves: **28**

Prep Time: **5** Minutes

Cook Time: **20** Minutes

Total Time: **25** Minutes

INGREDIENTS

- ½ cup jowar
- ½ cup onions
- 1 tsp sesame seeds
- pinch of salt
- ¼ tsp oil

DIRECTIONS

1. **In a bowl combine all ingredients together**
2. **Divide dough into 22-28 portions**
3. **Press each portion of dough between your hands until it looks like a thin circle**
4. **Grease a baking tray with oil**
5. **Bake for 18-20 minutes at 350 F**
6. **When ready remove and serve**

KALE CHIPS

Serves: **6**

Prep Time: **10** Minutes

Cook Time: **25** Minutes

Total Time: **35** Minutes

INGREDIENTS

- 1 bunch of kale
- 1 tablespoon olive oil
- 1 tsp salt

DIRECTIONS

1. Preheat the oven to 325 F
2. Chop the kale into chip size pieces
3. Put pieces into a bowl tops with olive oil and salt
4. Spread the leaves in a single layer onto a parchment paper
5. Bake for 20-25 minutes
6. When ready, remove and serve

CRANBERRY SALAD

Serves: **2**

Prep Time: **5** Minutes

Cook Time: **5** Minutes

Total Time: **10** Minutes

INGREDIENTS

- 1 can unsweetened pineapple
- 1 package cherry gelatin
- 1 tablespoon lemon juice
- ½ cup artificial sweetener
- 1 cup cranberries
- 1 orange
- 1 cup celery
- ½ cup pecans

DIRECTIONS

1. In a bowl mix all ingredients and mix well
2. Serve with dressing

ITALIAN SALAD

Serves: 2

Prep Time: 5 Minutes

Cook Time: 5 Minutes

Total Time: 10 Minutes

INGREDIENTS

- 8 oz. romaine lettuce
- 2 cups radicchio
- ¼ red onion
- 2 ribs celery
- 1 cup tomatoes
- 1 can chickpeas
- 1 cup salad dressing

DIRECTIONS

1. In a bowl mix all ingredients and mix well
2. Serve with dressing

CHICKPEA COLESLAW

Serves: 2
Prep Time: 5 Minutes
Cook Time: 5 Minutes
Total Time: 10 Minutes

INGREDIENTS

- 2 cans chickpeas
- 2 cups carrots
- 1 cup celery
- ¼ cup green onions
- ¼ cup dill leaves
- ¼ cup olive oil
- 1 cucumber
- 1 cup salad dressing

DIRECTIONS

1. In a bowl mix all ingredients and mix well
2. Serve with dressing

ROMAINE SALAD

Serves: 2

Prep Time: 5 Minutes

Cook Time: 5 Minutes

Total Time: 10 Minutes

INGREDIENTS

- 1 cup cooked quinoa
- 1 cup sunflower seeds
- 1 tablespoon olive oil
- 1 head romaine lettuce
- 1 cup carrots
- 1 cup cabbage
- ¼ cup radishes

DIRECTIONS

1. In a bowl mix all ingredients and mix well
2. Serve with dressing

GRAIN SALAD

Serves: 2

Prep Time: 5 Minutes

Cook Time: 5 Minutes

Total Time: 10 Minutes

INGREDIENTS

- 1 bunch coriander leaves
- 1 bunch mint leaves
- ¼ red onion
- 1 bunch parsley
- 1 cup lentils
- 1 tablespoon pumpkin seeds
- 1 tablespoon pine nuts

DIRECTIONS

1. In a bowl mix all ingredients and mix well
2. Serve with dressing

QUINOA SALAD

Serves: **2**

Prep Time: **5** Minutes

Cook Time: **5** Minutes

Total Time: **10** Minutes

INGREDIENTS

- **1 cauliflower**
- **2 cups cooked quinoa**
- **1 can chickpeas**
- **1 cup baby spinach**
- **¼ cup parsley**
- **¼ cup cilantro**
- **¼ cup green onion**
- **½ cup feta cheese**

DIRECTIONS

1. **In a bowl mix all ingredients and mix well**
2. **Serve with dressing**

WEDGE SALAD

Serves: **2**

Prep Time: **5** Minutes

Cook Time: **5** Minutes

Total Time: **10** Minutes

INGREDIENTS

- 1 head romaine lettuce
- 1 cup tomatoes
- 1 cup cucumber
- 1 cup celery
- ¼ cup olives
- 1 shallot
- 1 cup salad dressing

DIRECTIONS

1. **In a bowl mix all ingredients and mix well**
2. **Serve with dressing**

COUSCOUS SALAD

Serves: *2*

Prep Time: *5* Minutes

Cook Time: *5* Minutes

Total Time: *10* Minutes

INGREDIENTS

- 1 cup couscous
- ¼ cup pine nuts
- ¼ cup olive lil
- 1 tablespoon lemon juice
- 1 shallot
- 2 cloves garlic
- 1 tsp salt
- 1 can chickpeas
- 1 cup tomatoes
- ½ cup feta cheese
- 1 zucchini
- 1 tablespoon basil

DIRECTIONS

1. **In a bowl mix all ingredients and mix well**
2. **Serve with dressing**

FARRO SALAD

Serves: **2**

Prep Time: **5** Minutes

Cook Time: **5** Minutes

Total Time: **10** Minutes

INGREDIENTS

- 1 cup cooked FARRO
- 1 bay leaf
- 1 shallot
- ¼ cup olive oil
- 2 cups arugula
- ¼ cup parmesan cheese
- ¼ cup basil
- ¼ cup parsley
- ¼ cup pecans

DIRECTIONS

1. In a bowl mix all ingredients and mix well
2. Serve with dressing

THAI MANGO SALAD

Serves: 2
Prep Time: 5 Minutes
Cook Time: 5 Minutes
Total Time: 10 Minutes

INGREDIENTS

- 1 head leaf lettuce
- 1 red bell pepper
- 2 mangoes
- ¼ green onion
- ¼ cup peanuts
- ¼ cup cilantro
- 1 cup peanut dressing

DIRECTIONS

1. In a bowl mix all ingredients and mix well
2. Serve with dressing

LENTIL FRITATTA

Serves: **2**

Prep Time: **10** Minutes

Cook Time: **20** Minutes

Total Time: **30** Minutes

INGREDIENTS

- ½ lb. lentil
- 1 tablespoon olive oil
- ½ red onion
- ¼ tsp salt
- 2 eggs
- 2 oz. cheddar cheese
- 1 garlic clove
- ¼ tsp dill

DIRECTIONS

1. **In a bowl whisk eggs with salt and cheese**
2. **In a frying pan heat olive oil and pour egg mixture**
3. **Add remaining ingredients and mix well**
4. **Serve when ready**

SPINACH FRITATTA

Serves: 2
Prep Time: 10 Minutes
Cook Time: 20 Minutes
Total Time: 30 Minutes

INGREDIENTS

- ½ lb. spinach
- 1 tablespoon olive oil
- ½ red onion
- 2 eggs
- ¼ tsp salt
- 2 oz. cheddar cheese
- 1 garlic clove
- ¼ tsp dill

DIRECTIONS

1. In a skillet sauté spinach until tender
2. In a bowl whisk eggs with salt and cheese
3. In a frying pan heat olive oil and pour egg mixture
4. Add remaining ingredients and mix well
5. When ready serve with sautéed spinach

BLACK BEAN FRITATTA

Serves: **2**

Prep Time: **10** Minutes

Cook Time: **20** Minutes

Total Time: **30** Minutes

INGREDIENTS

- 1 cup cooked black beans
- 1 tablespoon olive oil
- ½ red onion
- ¼ tsp salt
- 2 oz. cheddar cheese
- 1 garlic clove
- ¼ tsp dill
- 2 eggs

DIRECTIONS

1. In a bowl whisk eggs with salt and cheese
2. In a frying pan heat olive oil and pour egg mixture
3. Add remaining ingredients and mix well
4. Serve when ready

CHEESE FRITATTA

Serves: **2**

Prep Time: **10** Minutes

Cook Time: **20** Minutes

Total Time: **30** Minutes

INGREDIENTS

- 1 tablespoon olive oil
- ½ red onion
- ¼ tsp salt
- 2 oz. cheddar cheese
- 1 garlic clove
- ¼ tsp dill
- 2 eggs

DIRECTIONS

1. In a bowl combine cheddar cheese and onion
2. In a frying pan heat olive oil and pour egg mixture
3. Add remaining ingredients and mix well
4. Serve when ready

BROCCOLI FRITATTA

Serves: **2**

Prep Time: **10** Minutes

Cook Time: **20** Minutes

Total Time: **30** Minutes

INGREDIENTS

- 1 cup broccoli
- 1 tablespoon olive oil
- ½ red onion
- ¼ tsp salt
- 2 oz. cheddar cheese
- 1 garlic clove
- 2 eggs
- ¼ tsp dill

DIRECTIONS

1. In a skillet sauté broccoli until tender
2. In a bowl whisk eggs with salt and cheese
3. In a frying pan heat olive oil and pour egg mixture
4. Add remaining ingredients and mix well
5. When ready serve with sautéed broccoli

SHAKSHUKA

Serves: **2**

Prep Time: **10** Minutes

Cook Time: **20** Minutes

Total Time: **30** Minutes

INGREDIENTS

- 1 tablespoon olive oil
- 1 red onion
- 1 red chili
- 1 garlic clove
- 2 cans cherry tomatoes
- 2 eggs

DIRECTIONS

1. In a frying pan cook garlic, chili, onions until soft
2. Stir in tomatoes and cook until mixture thickens
3. Crack the eggs over the sauce
4. Cover with a lid and cook for another 7-8 minutes
5. When ready remove from heat and serve

BROCCOLI CASSEROLE

Serves: **4**

Prep Time: **10** Minutes

Cook Time: **15** Minutes

Total Time: **25** Minutes

INGREDIENTS

- 1 onion
- 2 chicken breasts
- 2 tablespoons unsalted butter
- 2 eggs
- 2 cups cooked rice
- 2 cups cheese
- 1 cup parmesan cheese
- 2 cups cooked broccoli

DIRECTIONS

1. Sauté the veggies and set aside
2. Preheat the oven to 425 F
3. Transfer the sautéed veggies to a baking dish, add remaining ingredients to the baking dish
4. Mix well, add seasoning and place the dish in the oven
5. Bake for 12-15 minutes or until slightly brown
6. When ready remove from the oven and serve

BEAN FRITATTA

Serves: *2*

Prep Time: *10* Minutes

Cook Time: *20* Minutes

Total Time: *30* Minutes

INGREDIENTS

- 1 cup black beans
- 1 tablespoon olive oil
- ½ red onion
- 2 eggs
- ¼ tsp salt
- 2 oz. cheddar cheese
- 1 garlic clove
- ¼ tsp dill

DIRECTIONS

1. In a bowl whisk eggs with salt and cheese
2. In a frying pan heat olive oil and pour egg mixture
3. Add remaining ingredients and mix well
4. Serve when ready

ROASTED SQUASH

Serves: **3-4**

Prep Time: **10** Minutes

Cook Time: **20** Minutes

Total Time: **30** Minutes

INGREDIENTS

- 2 delicata squashes
- 2 tablespoons olive oil
- 1 tsp curry powder
- 1 tsp salt

DIRECTIONS

1. **Preheat the oven to 400 F**
2. **Cut everything in half lengthwise**
3. **Toss everything with olive oil and place onto a prepared baking sheet**
4. **Roast for 18-20 minutes at 400 F or until golden brown**
5. **When ready remove from the oven and serve**

POTATO CHIPS

Serves: 2

Prep Time: *10* Minutes

Cook Time: *20* Minutes

Total Time: *30* Minutes

INGREDIENTS

- 1 lb. sweet. potatoes
- 2 tablespoons olive oil
- 1 tablespoon smoked paprika
- 1 tablespoon salt

DIRECTIONS

1. Preheat the oven to 425 F
2. In a bowl toss everything with olive oil and seasoning
3. Spread everything onto a prepared baking sheet
4. Bake for 8-10 minutes or until crisp
5. When ready remove from the oven and serve

ZUCCHINI CHIPS

Serves: 2
Prep Time: 10 Minutes
Cook Time: 20 Minutes
Total Time: 30 Minutes

INGREDIENTS

- 1 lb. zucchini
- 2 tablespoons olive oil
- 1 tablespoon smoked paprika
- 1 tablespoon salt

DIRECTIONS

1. Preheat the oven to 425 F
2. In a bowl toss everything with olive oil and seasoning
3. Spread everything onto a prepared baking sheet
4. Bake for 8-10 minutes or until crisp
5. When ready remove from the oven and serve

PIZZA RECIPES

ZUCCHINI PIZZA CRUST

Serves: **4**

Prep Time: **10** Minutes

Cook Time: **30** Minutes

Total Time: **40** Minutes

INGREDIENTS

- 4 zucchinis
- 2 tsp salt
- 2 cups almond flour
- 2 tablespoons coconut flour
- 3 eggs
- 2 ½ cups cheddar cheese
- 1 tsp red pepper flakes
- 1 tsp dried oregano

DIRECTIONS

1. Shred the zucchini, sprinkle with salt and set aside
2. Preheat the oven to 400 F
3. Mix zucchini with remaining ingredients
4. Place the dough over a baking sheet and spread evenly

5. Pop the pizza crust in the oven for 30 minutes or until golden brown
6. When ready, remove and serve

BARBEQUE PIZZA

Serves: 2

Prep Time: 10 Minutes

Cook Time: 15 Minutes

Total Time: 25 Minutes

INGREDIENTS

- 1 pizza crust
- 1 tsp olive oil
- 1 cup onion
- ¼ cup red pepper strips
- 1 cup cooked chicken
- ¼ cup barbecue sauce
- 1 cup mozzarella cheese

DIRECTIONS

1. In a frying pan add pepper strips, onion and fry until soft
2. Add barbecue sauce, chicken and stir well
3. On a ready-made pizza crust spread onion, pepper mix, chicken and top with mozzarella
4. Bake for 12-15 minutes at 425 F

SHRIMP PIZZA

Serves: **4**

Prep Time: **5** Minutes

Cook Time: **20** Minutes

Total Time: **25** Minutes

INGREDIENTS

- 1 package pizza dough
- 1 tablespoon cornmeal
- 1/3 cup ricotta cheese
- 1 lb. shrimp
- 5 cloves roasted garlic
- 2 ¼ cups mozzarella cheese
- 1 tablespoon basil

DIRECTIONS

1. Stretch pizza dough across a baking pan and bake for 6-8 minutes, sprinkle cornmeal over the pan
2. Mix ricotta cheese, garlic, shrimp together and place over pizza crust
3. Cover pizza with mozzarella and basil
4. Bake for 12-15 minutes at 425 F

CAULIFLOWER CRUST PIZZA

Serves: **4**

Prep Time: **10** Minutes

Cook Time: **20** Minutes

Total Time: **30** Minutes

INGREDIENTS

- 1 lb. ground beef
- 1 egg
- 1 tsp parsley
- 1 tsp dried basil
- ¼ tsp salt
- ½ tsp pepper
- ¼ cup tomato puree
- 1 tsp tomato paste
- ¼ red pepper
- 1 tsp dried basil
- ¼ cup olives
- 5 slices prosciutto
- 4 oz. parmesan
- 1 handful fresh basil

DIRECTIONS

1. Preheat the oven to 430 F
2. In a bowl add salt, mince, egg, basil, pepper, parsley and mix well
3. Roll into a ball and place on a baking tray
4. Bake for 12-15 minutes
5. Mix the tomato paste with tomato puree and spread across the base
6. Top with peppers, prosciutto, parmesan, olives and bake for another 8-10 minutes
7. Remove from the oven, top with basil leaves and serve

THANK YOU FOR READING THIS BOOK!

CPSIA information can be obtained
at www.ICGtesting.com
Printed in the USA
BVHW071034040321
601714BV00005B/260